BANANAS!

Jacqueline Farmer

Illustrated by Page Eastburn O'Rourke

ini **Charlesbridge**

To my mother, who is always there with encouragement, help, and love.
—J. F.

For my bunch of boys: Kevin, Griffin, and Duncan.
—P. E. O'R.

Acknowledgments
"Bananananananananana" is copyrighted © 1977 by William Cole and is reprinted with permission. The jokes in this book are from *Biggest Riddle Book in the World*, copyright © 1976, and *The Zaniest Riddle Book in the World*, copyright © 1984, both written by Joseph Rosenbloom and reprinted with permission from Sterling Publishing. "Epitaph for Anna Hopewell" is from *Sudden and Awful: American Epitaphs*, copyright © 1968 by Stephen Greene Press. "Or Was She Pushed" is from *A Book of Humorous Limericks*, copyright © 1926 by Hudleman-Julius Company.

Library of Congress Cataloging-in-Publication Data
Farmer, Jacqueline.
    Bananas!/Jacqueline Farmer; illustrated by Page Eastburn O'Rourke.
        p.   cm.
    Summary: Describes the growth, distribution, history, and nutritional value of the banana. Includes recipes, poems, and jokes.
      ISBN 0-88106-114-X (reinforced for library use)
      ISBN 0-88106-115-8 (softcover)
1. Bananas—Juvenile literature. 2. Cookery (Bananas)—Juvenile literature. [1. Bananas.] I. Title.
SB379.B2F27   1999
641.3'4772—dc21   99-19223

Printed in South Korea
(hc) 10 9 8 7 6 5 4 3 2 1
(sc) 10 9 8 7 6 5 4 3 2 1

Published by Charlesbridge Publishing
85 Main Street, Watertown, MA 02472
(617) 926-0329
www.charlesbridge.com

The illustrations in this book were done in watercolor on Arches watercolor paper.
The display type and text type were set in Guthrie Plain and Stone Sans Serif.
Color separations were made by Sung In Printing, Inc., South Korea.
Printed and bound by Sung In Printing, Inc., South Korea
Production supervision by Brian G. Walker
Designed by Diane M. Earley

Introducing the one, the only, banana!

The banana is an intriguing fruit that's loved around the world. It's the most popular fruit in America, where each person eats an average of twenty-eight pounds of bananas annually. Now that's a bunch of bananas!

Why are we all bananas for bananas? Well, simply put, the banana is an extraordinary fruit. It grows on a unique plant that has been cultivated for centuries. It's shipped carefully to arrive in perfect condition. It's nutritious and delicious, and its funny appearance makes us laugh!

The banana lives life in the fast lane!

Thousands of years ago, bananas were one of the first fruits ever grown on farms. Today huge commercial banana farms, called plantations, are found in many tropical areas. Though bananas grow best in tropical warmth, a few determined farmers in Iceland have successfully grown bananas in soil heated by geysers.

Still, the banana plant thrives where it's hot and humid. With water, sun, and good drainage, it sprouts just like Jack's bean stalk . . . very, very fast. A banana plant can grow up to thirty feet tall in a single year!

A banana plant grows from either a sucker or a rhizome. Suckers are small banana plants that sprout around the main plant. Banana farmers cut most of them down with a large knife called a machete, leaving the strongest suckers to grow into new plants.

Each banana plant has a fat, bulblike root called a rhizome. It has "eyes" on it just like a potato. If the farmer cuts the rhizome into pieces and plants them, a new banana plant will grow from each of the eyes.

Most people think bananas grow on trees. But even though the banana plant looks like a tree, it's really the world's largest herb. This means that the banana plant does not have a woody trunk. Fat leaves, some as long as twelve feet, spiral upward from the ground. Wrapping around one another, they form a sturdy stem that holds the plant upright.

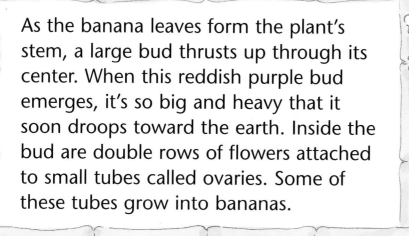

As the banana leaves form the plant's stem, a large bud thrusts up through its center. When this reddish purple bud emerges, it's so big and heavy that it soon droops toward the earth. Inside the bud are double rows of flowers attached to small tubes called ovaries. Some of these tubes grow into bananas.

New bananas look like fingers, and that's what they are called. Each group of ten to twenty is called a hand. A single plant can produce as many as fifteen hands, forming a bunch that can weigh more than one hundred pounds!

Banana farmers have to work very hard. They make sure that the plants have enough water and fertilizer, and they wrap the developing fruit in plastic sleeves to protect it against damage by birds, insects, and bad weather.

Some plants produce so much fruit that farmers use poles and twine to keep the stalks upright.

Most bananas must be cut from the stalk while unripe. If left on the plant to ripen, the fruit can burst its skin. When the peel splits, the banana spoils.

Bananas are good sports!

The banana plant sometimes produces a new variety for no apparent reason. This surprising process is called sporting. A dramatic example of a really "good sport" occurred in 1836 when yellow bananas first appeared. Originally bananas were only red and green. The new yellow variety, discovered on the island of Jamaica, was so sweet and delicious that it soon became wildly popular.

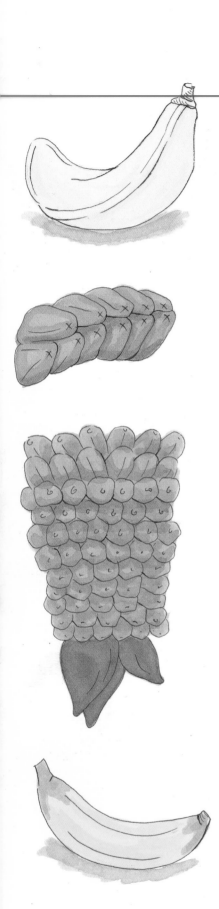

Many other "good sports" have appeared. Over five hundred different kinds of bananas exist today. The plantain, the Hawaiian Red, and the Cavendish are the varieties found in most stores.

Rhino Horn Banana: This banana from East Africa can grow two feet long. It really looks like the horn of a rhinoceros.

Praying Hands Banana: The fingers of these bananas from Indonesia are stuck together to form a single hand. The fruit inside the skin is separate, though.

Thousand Finger Banana: Wow! This banana from Honduras produces fruit for up to five months, until there are almost too many bananas to count. Compare this with other varieties' average fruiting period of just two to three months.

Cavendish: These yellow bananas grow in the Caribbean and in Central and South America. The Cavendish is the banana most commonly sold in the United States today.

Go San Heong Banana: This very sweet banana from southern China is also very fragrant. Its name means "You can smell it from over the next mountain." Fortunately it smells good!

Hawaiian Red: This banana has many names: Indio, Cuban Red, and Morado, just to name a few. Ancient Hawaiian royal families once decreed that red bananas were taboo for commoners. *Taboo* then became another name for this variety.

Ice Cream or **Blue Java:** This yummy banana is bluish when unripe. When ready to eat, its sweet snow-white flesh melts in your mouth and tastes like banana ice cream!

Plantain: This large relative of the banana probably originated in southern India. When the plantain is green it's used mostly for cooking. When the peel turns black the fruit isn't spoiled. That's when the raw flesh is the sweetest.

Some people say that banana plantations are bad for the environment and for people. Many rainforest trees are cut down when these giant farms are built, workers are exposed to insecticides on the job, and some fruit companies pay their workers very low wages.

Responsible companies are working hard to correct these problems. They are replanting native trees, trying new techniques to reduce the use of pesticides, and allowing plantation workers to form unions. More steps like these will help make banana farming safe for both the environment and for people.

Make way for bananas!

Bananas need to be babied as they journey to your kitchen table. They are very delicate and bruise easily. The trip begins on the plantation, where workers carefully cut the fruit from the plant. The bananas are hung on sturdy moving cables that carry them to a processing plant. There the bunches are separated into the small clusters you see in the store, washed, inspected, and packed into special boxes.

Next the forty-pound boxes are loaded onto refrigerated ships. These **enormous** ships can carry between 150,000 and 200,000 boxes of bananas. That adds up to almost eight million pounds of bananas!

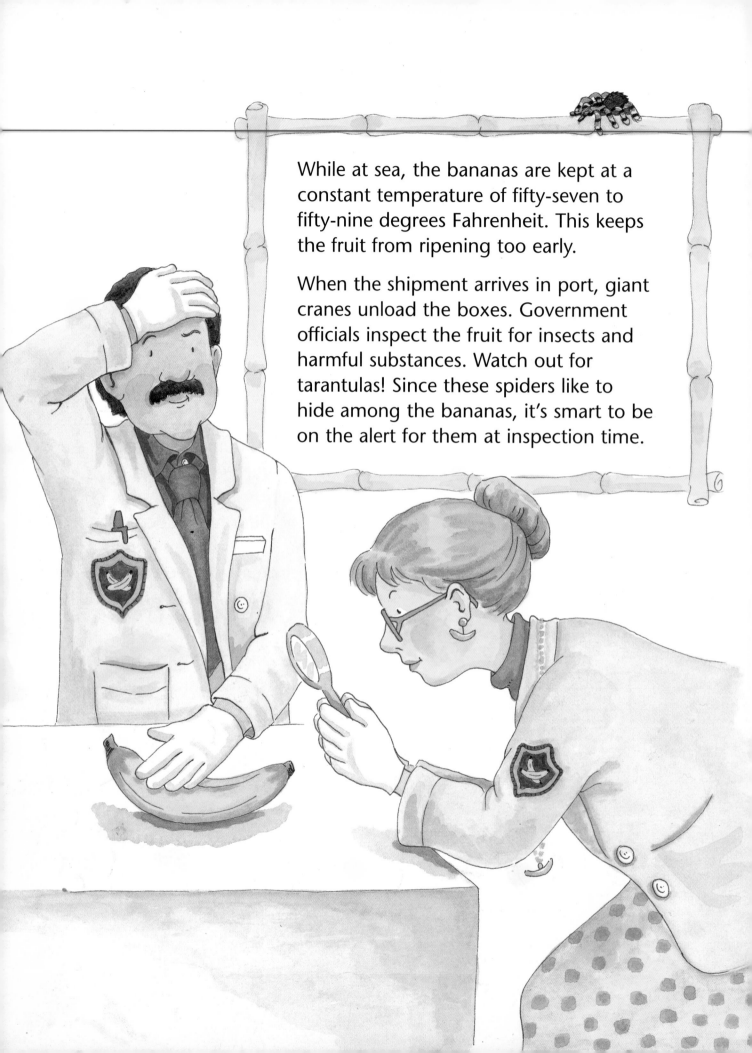

While at sea, the bananas are kept at a constant temperature of fifty-seven to fifty-nine degrees Fahrenheit. This keeps the fruit from ripening too early.

When the shipment arrives in port, giant cranes unload the boxes. Government officials inspect the fruit for insects and harmful substances. Watch out for tarantulas! Since these spiders like to hide among the bananas, it's smart to be on the alert for them at inspection time.

Next the fruit is kept in special ripening rooms for three and one-half to seven days. There the internal temperature of the bananas is gradually raised. When the time is right, refrigerated trucks deliver the bananas to their final destinations: schools, hospitals, supermarkets, or zoos.

Bananas have an ancient and illustrious past!

The earliest banana probably grew in an area we now call the Malay Archipelago, and the plant soon spread to other parts of Southeast Asia.

In 327 B.C.E. Alexander the Great invaded India and saw his first banana. He feared it might be poisonous until he saw an Indian man eating one. He took a bite himself and decided he liked it! He then recorded for history that "wise men in India sat in the shade of a banana tree and enjoyed its fruit." Years later, botanists named the banana *Musa sapientum,* or "fruit of the wise."

Travelers carried the banana from Asia to Africa. It received many different names along the way. In Burma, now called Myanmar, it was given the name *hnget pyaw*. This means "the birds told." Burmese legend explains that people knew the banana was safe to eat when they saw birds eating it.

When Portuguese sailors visited Guinea, a country on the West African coast, they enjoyed *banemas*. This Guinian word for the fruit soon became *banana*, the English word we use today.

In the early 1500s Spanish missionary Friar Tomas de Berlanga carried a banana plant all the way from the Canary Islands to the island of Santo Domingo in the West Indies. He just **loved** bananas! Before long he built the first banana plantation in the Americas.

CURIOSITY OF THE Indies

INTRODUCING The Phone A.G.Bell

10¢ each

At the United States Centennial Exhibition in Philadelphia in 1876, two exciting discoveries were displayed. Inventor Alexander Graham Bell introduced the telephone, while savvy businessmen sold a new, exotic fruit from the Caribbean called the banana. The rest is history!

Americans at the 1876 Centennial Exhibition developed a taste for bananas. Customers were ready to buy them . . . but few were available for purchase!

The earliest efforts to ship bananas failed, but by the early twentieth century shipbuilders had built refrigerated ships. They painted them white to reflect the hot tropical sun. In 1907 this "Great White Fleet" was ready to set sail. The fruit sold like hotcakes—bananas were big business!

Some animals munch a bunch for lunch!

Many creatures that live in tropical areas love to eat bananas. The macaw, a long-tailed parrot from Central and South America, uses the four powerful clawed toes on each foot to grasp its banana of choice.

The chimpanzee from Africa is quite skilled at using its hands and feet to hold and peel ripe bananas. The peels and unripe fruit that are tossed to the forest floor become dinner for insects and small animals.

The owl butterfly, *Caligo eurilochus*, from Central and South American rain forests, also feeds on the banana. This creature is not content with ripe fruit, however. Its banana of choice is rotten! The fermented banana juice it drinks has caused more than one owl butterfly to wobble in flight.

At night other creatures stop by to eat. A nocturnal primate from Africa, the Allen bush baby, feasts on leftovers that have fallen to the ground. Another banana lover is *Otheris fullonia*, the Pacific fruit-piercing moth. This insect has a long, strong mouth that easily pierces the banana's tough skin.

Can a banana a day keep the doctor away?

We've all heard the saying about the apple, but how does the banana compare? This chart shows the nutritional value of a six-ounce apple and a six-ounce banana.

	Apple	Banana
Calories	100	128
Iron	0.3 mg	1.1 mg
Phosphorus	12 mg	39 mg
Potassium	196 mg	555 mg
Vitamin A	90 IU	285 IU
Vitamin B$_6$	0.08 mg	0.77 mg
Vitamin C	10 mg	15 mg
Magnesium	8.5 mg	49.5 mg
Niacin	1.1 mg	1.0 mg

Clearly, the banana's a winner!

The banana is the perfect fast food. It's easy to carry in a lunch box, and it's really easy to eat. It's also very nutritious. A single banana contains 25 percent of the U.S. Recommended Daily Allowance of vitamin B_6, which strengthens red blood cells, and 15 percent of the recommended amount of vitamin C, which keeps the organs of the body healthy.

The banana also contains pectin, which helps form a gel that carries waste out of the body. Pectin also helps lower the body's cholesterol level and heal ulcers. Because bananas are very easy to digest, they make wonderful baby food, too.

Bananas can provide much of the potassium the body needs each day to keep muscles strong and healthy. Marathon runners love them and often have to dodge the peels tossed on the roadway by runners ahead of them.

Even though bananas are known to increase energy, they also contain an amino acid, called tryptophan, that is thought to make people sleepy. Enjoying the fruit at bedtime is said to help you fall asleep. No, not by counting bananas —by **eating** them!

So now you know that you should eat lots of bananas, but how do you do it politely? Americans who purchased the foil-wrapped bananas at the 1876 Centennial Exhibition ate them with knives and forks! Soon etiquette books had instructions on banana manners for those who cared about such things. Americans were told to peel the fruit, lay it on a plate, cut it into small pieces with a fruit knife, and eat it with a fruit fork.

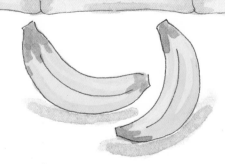

A banana treat . . .

Children all over the world enjoy banana snacks. In the Caribbean they eat *tostones*, which are slices of plantain that are fried and seasoned with salt and other spices. *Tostones* are not sweet at all, but they taste delicious!

Indian children might enjoy banana chutney with their dinner. Chutney is a spicy type of relish that is often served with Indian food. Indian families sometimes use banana leaves as plates.

Banana Chutney

3 very ripe bananas (1 $\frac{1}{2}$ cups mashed)
2 tablespoons fresh lemon juice
2 teaspoons freshly grated lemon rind
2 pinches ground cloves
sugar as needed

Mash bananas in small saucepan. Stir in lemon juice, rind, and cloves. With an adult's help, boil mixture. Stir on low heat for fifteen minutes. Pour into clean jar and refrigerate. Eat with dinner or on toast for breakfast.

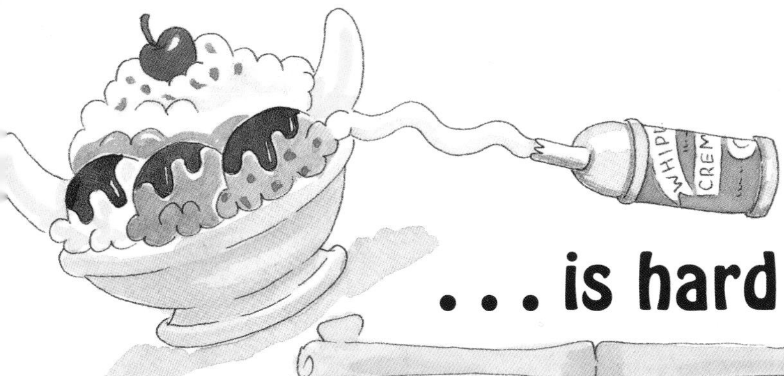

. . . is hard to beat!

In Asian countries the banana flower is added to salads, and in other tropical areas banana fritters are a popular dessert. To make fritters, soak pieces of banana in sweetened lime juice, dip them in batter, and then deep-fry them. Yummy!

Why not try banana chocolate-chip pancakes? Just add small chunks of banana and a few chocolate chips to the batter before cooking.

This next banana treat has been a favorite for about one hundred years.

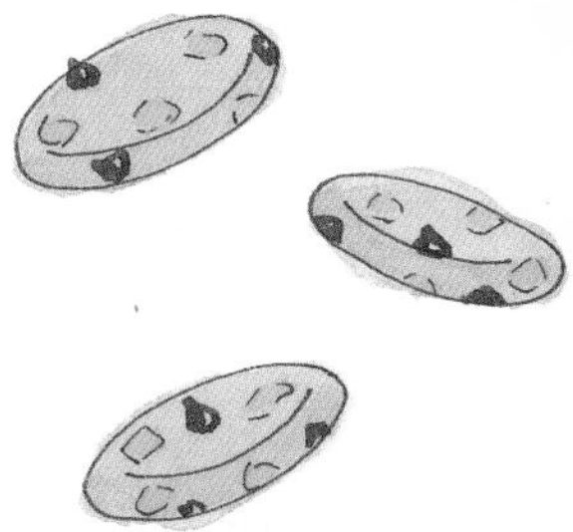

Banana Split
1 medium banana
1 scoop vanilla ice cream
1 scoop strawberry ice cream
1 scoop chocolate ice cream
chocolate sauce
strawberry sauce
marshmallow crème
whipped cream
nuts
cherry

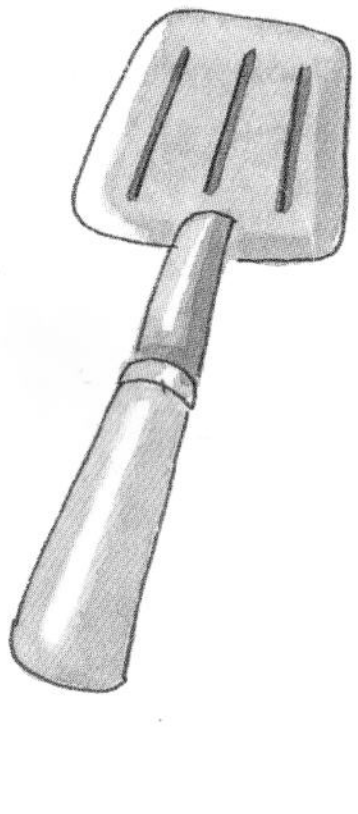

Assemble as shown in the picture above and enjoy!

Let's try a few more bananadanadelicious snacks.

Chocolate-dipped Bananas

6 ripe bananas, peeled
$\frac{1}{2}$ cup semisweet chocolate pieces
$\frac{1}{4}$ cup evaporated milk
12 craft sticks

Cut bananas in half crosswise. Push stick into cut ends and freeze for an hour. Have an adult help melt chocolate and evaporated milk in a saucepan over low heat. While still warm, pour mixture into shallow pan. Twirl frozen bananas in chocolate to coat. Eat right away or wrap in foil and freeze for later.

Frosted Banana Milk Shake

1 small, very ripe banana
1 cup milk
$\frac{1}{4}$ teaspoon vanilla
1 large scoop vanilla or strawberry ice cream
cinnamon or nutmeg

Mash banana and put into blender. Add milk, vanilla, and ice cream. With an adult helping, blend well. Pour into glass and top with cinnamon or nutmeg.

Did you hear the one about the banana?

There are lots of silly banana songs, riddles, poems, and limericks. There are even a few banana epitaphs (tributes on gravestones). Here's some banana humor to tickle your funny bone.

Banananananananana
I thought I'd win the spelling bee
And get right to the top
But I started to spell "banana"
And I didn't know when to stop.
—William Cole

Q: Why did the banana go out with the prune?
A: Because it couldn't get a date.

Time flies like an arrow.
Fruit flies like a banana.
—Groucho Marx

Epitaph for Anna Hopewell Enosburg, Vermont
Here lies the body of our Anna,
Done to death by a banana.
It wasn't the fruit that laid her low,
But the skin of the thing that made her go.

Q: Why is a banana peel on the sidewalk like music?
A: *Because if you don't C-sharp you'll B-flat.*

Or Was She Pushed?
There was a young lady named Hannah,
Who slipped on a peel of banana.
As she lay on her side,
More stars she espied
Than there are in the Star-Spangled Banner.

Q: What does the banana do when it sees a gorilla?
A: *The banana splits!*

Q: Why do bananas use suntan lotion?
A: *Because they peel.*

Banana Tip 1: To ripen a banana quickly at home, enclose it in a paper bag with a tomato or an apple. The fruits' natural gases, in addition to the darkness, should ripen the banana overnight.

Silly Song Titles
"My Brother Thinks He's a Banana"
"Bananaphone"
"When Banana Skins Are Falling"
"A Shoe with No Lace, a Banana with No Skin"
"30,000 Pounds of Bananas"

Q: What do you get when you cross a couple of bananas?
A: *A pair of slippers.*

Q: Did you hear the joke about the banana peel?
A: *Sorry, it must have slipped my mind.*

Q: What do you get when you cross a banana and a comedian?
A: *Peels of laughter.*

Banana Tip 2: Most people don't refrigerate bananas. The cold makes the skin turn black and the fruit stop ripening.

World Record
The record for the world's longest banana split was set in 1988 at 4.55 miles in Selinsgrove, Pennsylvania.

4.55 MILES

So why bananas?

The banana is special in the way it grows: up to thirty feet tall with no woody trunk. It's also special for its many unique varieties—just imagine a banana that tastes like ice cream! The banana was one of the first fruits ever grown on a farm, and it's also really nutritious. Don't you love that potassium and pectin?

Animals and insects think the banana is pretty neat, too. And what other fruit could make us laugh so much? But really, the proof is in the pudding (banana pudding, of course). The banana is special because it **tastes so good!**